BEHIND THE SCENES
AT THE OLYMPICS

D1304709

By Joanne and James Mattern

Perfection Learning®

About the Authors

Joanne Mattern is the author of many books for children. She especially likes writing nonfiction because it allows her to bring real people, places, and events to life. "I firmly believe that everything in the world is a story waiting to be told."

Along with writing, Joanne enjoys speaking to school and community groups about the topics in her books. She is also a huge baseball fan and enjoys music and needlework.

Joanne's husband, James, enjoys all sports. He is especially interested in sports history, trivia, and statistics.

Joanne and James live in the Hudson Valley of New York State with their young daughter. The family also includes a greyhound and two cats. "More animals are always welcome!"

Design: Emily J. Greazel

Image Credits:
© AFP/CORBIS cover, pp. 32, 61; © Wally McNamee/CORBIS pp. 5, 47; © Bettmann/CORBIS pp. 17, 52-53; © Mike King/CORBIS p. 31; © Kevin Flemming/CORBIS pp. 34-35; © Carl and Ann Purcell/CORBIS p. 37; © Reuters New/Media Inc./CORBIS p. 43.

ArtToday (some images copyright www.arttoday.com) pp. 6, 8, 9, 10, 11, 13, 14, 15, 19, 23, 24, 28 (bottom), 29, 38, 39, 41, 44, 45, 46, 48, 50, 57; Corel Professional Photos pp. 20-21, 26, 27, 55.

For information, contact Perfection Learning® Corporation,
1000 North Second Avenue,
P.O. Box 500, Logan, Iowa 51546-0500.
Tel: 1-800-831-4190 • Fax: 1-800-543-2745
perfectionlearning.com
PB ISBN-10: 0-7891-5860-4 ISBN-13: 978-0-7891-5860-4
RLB ISBN-10: 0-7569-0981-3 ISBN-13: 978-0-7569-0981-9

3 4 5 6 7 8 PP 13 12 11 10 09 08

TABLE OF CONTENTS

Introduction

Every two years, athletes from all over the world gather for the Olympic Games. They take part in many different sports, from swimming to basketball, ice-skating to skiing. The winners are given medals to honor their accomplishments. They win respect and praise for themselves, their teams, and their countries. Millions of people around the world watch the Games. They marvel at the athletes' incredible feats.

Sports are the main focus of the Olympics. Yet, many other elements are needed for the Games. The Olympics bring athletes from dozens of nations into one host city. Choosing that city and getting it ready is a huge effort. It takes many years and a lot of money.

Sometimes politics and violence interfere with athletic competition. Throughout the history of the modern Games, they have been touched and changed by wars, **terrorist** acts, **boycotts**, and other political demonstrations.

Some athletes want to be the best. They often use drugs to improve their performance. This practice hurts the honor of the Games. And it changes the way athletes perform.

For better or worse, the Olympic Games are much more than just athletic events. Let's go behind the scenes and take a look at how the Olympics came to be and how they work in the modern world.

CHAPTER ONE

The Ancient Olympics

The Olympics and the Gods

The Olympics began about 2,770 years ago in ancient Greece. Greece was a place where athletic ability was very important. Writings and paintings from those long-ago days describe different athletic contests. These included footraces, horse races, and boat races.

The Greeks believed in many different gods and heroes. The most important god was Zeus, who lived on Mount Olympus.

Zeus

The original Games were actually a religious festival to honor Zeus and other gods. The winners were considered special people touched by the gods. Sports also helped young men stay fit and ready to fight in the many battles of those days.

The Olympics were not the only sports festival in ancient Greece. They were part of the Panhellenic Games. These were open to anyone who lived in Greece. There were four different games—the Pythian, the Nemean, the Isthmian, and the Olympics. Each honored a different god. The Games alternated, so a different one was held each year.

Events

The first recorded Olympics were held in 776 B.C. at Olympia. Olympia was a religious shrine dedicated to Zeus. Competitors came from Greek **city-states**. At that time, the Olympics consisted of just one event—the *stade*. The stade was a short footrace of about 630 feet. The first recorded champion was a man named Coroebos of Elis.

fun fact

Coroebos was not a professional athlete. He was actually a cook!

fun fact

Our word *stadium* comes from the Greek word *stade*. A stadium is a large structure containing a field surrounded by rows of seats. It is a place where sports events are held.

The Games were held once every four years. In 724 B.C., a second race was added. This race was the *diaulus*. It was about 1,260 feet long. Four years later, a longer race, the *dolichus*, took place. This race was between 2½ and 3 miles long.

None of these races was run on a circular track as they are today. Instead, the athletes ran in a straight line to a post. Once there, they turned around and ran back.

Chariot race

As the years passed, more events were added. These included the **pentathlon**, chariot racing, horse racing, boxing, running in armor, and a combination of boxing and wrestling called *pankration*. All these events were for individuals. Team events weren't held in the ancient Games.

The ancient Olympics were held in a huge stadium. **Archaeologists** think that the stadium held about 40,000 people.

A Different Kind of Olympics

The events weren't the only difference from today's Games. Another difference was the participants. All the athletes were men! Women were not allowed to take part. In fact, they weren't even allowed to watch the Games!

fun fact

Pankration was a brutal sport in which almost any type of fighting was allowed. Some athletes were killed while competing in this event.

Although women couldn't compete in the Olympics, they did have their own competitions. Every four years, a women's sports festival, the Heraia, was held at Olympia. The Heraia honored the goddess Hera, Zeus's wife. However, the only event at the Heraia was a short footrace.

Another difference between the ancient Games and the modern Olympics was what the athletes wore. Today's athletes wear specially designed clothing. In the early days, the athletes wore shorts. But starting around 720 B.C., they performed nude.

fun fact

Even though women couldn't take part in the Games, they could still be winners. The winner of the chariot race was not the driver. It was the owner of the horses. Women were allowed to own horses in those days. But they could not race them. So a woman could be a chariot-racing champ!

Footrace

Today's athletes receive gold, silver, or bronze medals for their achievements. In ancient Greece, only the winner of an event was recognized. And the champions received much simpler prizes. They were presented with olive wreaths to wear on their heads. They also were invited to a feast. Olympic winners became heroes and were treated as important men for the rest of their lives.

Olive wreath

fun fact

Ancient poems said that the wreaths came from an olive tree that had been planted by the Greek hero Hercules.

The ancient Games were also shorter than the modern Games. Until 692 B.C., all the events were held in one day. Later, the Games lasted longer. Finally, they became a five-day festival.

The ancient Greeks valued the Olympic Games so much that they didn't let anything stop them. If the city-states were at war, they stopped fighting for one month. This was called the Sacred Truce. The Sacred Truce was not just a symbol of the Games' importance. It also allowed athletes and spectators to travel to the Games safely.

Chariot race winner receiving olive wreaths

A Five-Day Festival

People traveled from all parts of Greece to see the Olympics. The roads were crowded weeks before the festival. People walked, rode horses, or traveled in carriages.

Meanwhile, barges carried princes and other important citizens up the river to Olympia. Some of these princes came from Italy, Africa, and other parts of the world. The only people missing from the arriving crowds were the athletes. They had been in Olympia for a month, training and preparing for the Games.

No athletic events were held on the first day of the Games. Instead, everyone attended a religious ceremony at the temple of Zeus. Here the athletes promised to compete fairly. The judges also took an oath to make fair and honest decisions. Finally, a list of the competitors and their events was posted on a white board.

fun fact

All the Olympic judges wore purple robes so people would know who they were.

Athletes weren't the only ones who competed for a place at the Games. On the first day, trumpeters and **heralds** competed to see which of them would take part. It was a great honor to be the trumpeter who signaled the start of a race or the herald who announced the winners.

The crowds at the Olympics had a lot to do that first day. The streets were filled with musicians, dancers, magicians, and poets. Food vendors and other **peddlers** set up tents outside the stadium. Visitors also toured the temples, museums, and other important buildings at Olympia. And they enjoyed seeing princes, philosophers, and other famous men in the crowds, just as we enjoy watching celebrities today!

The competitions began on the second day. That's when the chariot race was run.

The chariot race was held at the hippodrome, a racing **arena**. The hippodrome was a large, flat rectangle at the edge of Olympia. The racecourse was a straight track with turning posts at either end. The race was just over 5 miles long, or 24 times around the track.

As the chariots raced around the turns, they often bumped into one another. Head-on collisions were frequent because there were no barriers between chariots racing in opposite directions.

Chariot races held at the racing arena

Horse races were also held at the hippodrome on the second day. Horses ran twice the length of the track, about a half mile.

Riders did not use saddles or stirrups. So they were often thrown from their horses. If a horse crossed the finish line without its rider, often it would be declared the winner.

The final event of the second day was the pentathlon. This event was held in the stadium. Athletes had to throw a **discus** and a **javelin**, perform a long jump while carrying heavy **dumbbells** in their hands, race the length of the stadium, and wrestle.

The third day started with a sacrifice to Zeus. Athletes, priests, and government representatives marched to the temple. There, they sacrificed 100 bulls and left valuable gifts, such as gold and silver.

After the sacrifice, the boys held their competitions. Boys competed in wrestling and the stade. Later, in 616 B.C., a boxing match was added.

Most of the events were held on the fourth day. There were three footraces—the dolichus, the diaulus, and the men's stade. A race in armor, the pankration, wrestling, and boxing matches were also held on that day.

fun fact

If a boxer was killed during a match, he was declared the winner!

Athletic competitions weren't held on the fifth and last day. In the morning, the judges, winning athletes, and important guests marched to the temple of Zeus. At this time, each champion received an olive wreath. The statue of Zeus was also crowned with olive leaves. This showed his triumph over all the other gods.

After the procession, a great feast was held to honor the winning athletes. Finally, all the athletes and spectators packed up their things and began the long journey home.

Feasts similar to this were held in honor of the winning athletes.

The Olympics Change . . . and Fade Away

Around the year 150 A.D., Rome conquered Greece. The Olympic Games continued, but things began to change. Instead of olive wreaths, winners were awarded money. This led to cheating.

Cities hired **professional** athletes so they would have a better chance of winning. They also paid **bribes** to the judges. One boxer, Eupolus of Thessaly, even bribed three opponents to lose their matches!

Some athletes were fined for bribery and other misbehavior. The money from the fines was used to build several statues on top of the stadium.

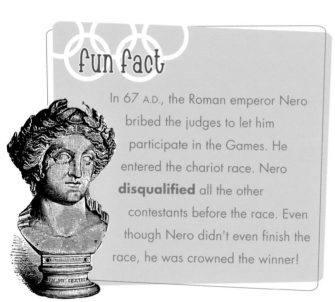

fun fact

In 67 A.D., the Roman emperor Nero bribed the judges to let him participate in the Games. He entered the chariot race. Nero **disqualified** all the other contestants before the race. Even though Nero didn't even finish the race, he was crowned the winner!

After 261 A.D., records of Olympic winners couldn't be found. So historians aren't sure if the Games were still held on a regular schedule. The Olympics stopped for good in 394 A.D. That's when a Roman emperor named Theodosius I banned the Games. Theodosius was a Christian. He didn't want the Olympics to be held because they honored Greek gods.

Olympia was abandoned, and the Olympics were forgotten. An invading army destroyed the stadium of Olympia. Then earthquakes and floods buried it under 15 feet of mud and dirt for more than a thousand years.

CHAPTER TWO

Starting Over: The Modern Olympics

For more than one thousand years, the world forgot about the Olympics. But people still enjoyed sports and competitions.

Sports and Schools

During the 1800s, students in Great Britain studied ancient Latin and Greek literature and history. Sports were also an important part of British education. Like the ancient Greeks, the British thought that sports were a good way to build character, self-confidence, and strength. Schools in other countries also began focusing on sports as an important part of life and learning.

At about this time, the ancient site of the Olympic Games was discovered.

Englishman Richard Chandler first discovered Olympia in 1766. In 1829, a team of French archaeologists explored the site. But they didn't have enough time to make many discoveries.

Finally, between 1875 and 1881, a team of German scholars and archaeologists **excavated** almost all the buildings at Olympia. They also found more than 130 statues and 6000 other objects.

One of the people who read about the German archaeologists and their work was French nobleman Baron Pierre de Coubertin. Coubertin was inspired by the ideals of the ancient Olympic Games. He decided to **revive** the Olympics. He planned to open them to athletes from all over the world.

Baron Pierre de Coubertin

Pierre de Coubertin was born on January 1, 1863. When he was just eight years old, France was badly defeated by Germany in the Franco-Prussian War. Coubertin wondered if France lost because French soldiers weren't physically fit. Unlike British and German students, French children didn't spend much time playing sports.

For the rest of his life, Coubertin worked to promote physical fitness. He traveled around the world. He visited British and American schools and studied their sports programs. He felt that introducing sports to French schools would be good for the students and the country.

Baron Pierre de Coubertin

Coubertin also felt that sports could promote world peace. Athletic contests were a peaceful way for nations to compete against one another. And if a nation's young men were busy preparing for sporting events, they wouldn't be able to fight as soldiers.

In 1892, Coubertin gave a speech in Paris. He explained his ideas for a revival of the Olympic Games. Coubertin received great public support for his idea.

Two years later, Coubertin organized an international sports conference in Paris. At that meeting, sports-minded people from 13 countries laid the foundation for the modern Olympics. They also founded the International Olympic Committee (IOC).

The IOC

The IOC is a group of people who oversee the Olympic Games and encourage **amateur** sports. All IOC members are private citizens. They do not represent specific governments. This allows the IOC to remain free of political influences and disagreements.

To join the IOC, a person must be invited by the members. An IOC member has to be a well-known supporter of amateur athletics. Members can serve until they are 72 years old. A new member is invited to join only when a member dies or resigns.

Reconstruction of Athens' Stadium

Coubertin went to the Crown Prince of Greece with his plan to revive the Olympics. The Crown Prince liked the plan. Coubertin hoped to hold the Games at Olympia where the ancient Games had been held. But the site was not suitable for athletic competitions. Instead, Athens, Greece, was chosen to host the first modern Olympic Games in 1896.

fun fact

The ruins of an ancient stadium in Athens were rebuilt in marble to host the 1896 Olympics. Greek George Averoff paid $360,000 to restore the stadium.

The Early Olympics

The first modern Olympics were very small. Thirteen countries participated. Of the 311 athletes, 230 were from Greece!

Competitors were mostly members of athletic clubs or college teams. The American team was made up of ten track-and-field athletes, two pistol shooters, and one swimmer. The American track-and-field team easily won nine events. But the Greeks won the most medals with 47.

Huge crowds turned out to see 42 events in nine different sports. These first modern Olympics lasted for ten days.

Athens wanted to host the Olympics every four years. Coubertin insisted that every major city in the world should have a chance to be a host city. He wanted the Games to be an international event, not a Greek competition.

fun fact

The first American Olympic team was made up of students from Harvard, Princeton, and Yale Universities.

Modern Olympic Stadium, Athens, Greece

The second modern Olympics were held in Paris, France, in 1900. This city was chosen because Coubertin was French. However, these Games were disorganized and poorly attended.

Another problem was that the Olympics were held as part of the Paris International Exhibition. This meant that the Games were stretched out over five months instead of just a few days.

During the Exhibition, other sporting events were taking place. In the confusion, some athletes didn't even realize they were competing in the Olympic Games!

The 1904 Olympics also had problems. They were originally scheduled for Chicago. But organizers of the World's Fair in St. Louis, Missouri, demanded that the Olympics be held there as part of the fair. The IOC agreed.

fun fact

Women competed for the first time in the 1900 Olympics. They played tennis and golf. These Olympics were also the first to feature team sports. At the 1896 Olympics, all the events had been for individuals.

Unfortunately, it was hard for European athletes to travel across the Atlantic Ocean to the middle of the United States. Because of this, almost all the competitors were from the United States or Canada. Many events featured competitions between different American clubs or universities. In fact, the only non-American winner was Ireland's Thomas Kiely. He won the **decathlon**.

After the problems at the 1900 and 1904 Games, people lost interest in the Olympics. Then the "Interim Games" were held in Athens in 1906. These unofficial Games were well-run and very successful. The public became interested in the Olympics again and looked forward to the next Games.

The 1908 Olympics were held in London. These Games had problems too. The United States and Sweden were angry when their flags weren't flown at the stadium. Finland refused to march under the flag of Russia. Russia ruled Finland at that time. The weather was terrible. Heavy rain led to difficult conditions for the cycling races and tennis matches.

Even worse, the British judges were accused of breaking rules so British athletes would win. It was later decided that future competitions would be overseen by an international team of judges instead of judges from the host country.

Fortunately, the Olympics became better organized and more popular as the years went by. The 1912 Olympics were held in Stockholm, Sweden. They were a model of good sportsmanship and exciting performances.

fun fact

The 1908 Olympics were supposed to be held in Rome, Italy. But in 1906, the Italian volcano Mount Vesuvius erupted. It cost so much money to repair the damage that Italy had to back out of hosting the Games.

Mount Vesuvius

1930s Olympics—Javelin

**1936 Olympic Games,
opening day, Berlin**

Beginning in 1924, separate Olympics were held for winter sports and summer sports. At first, organizers planned to have the Summer and Winter Games in the same city. However, they soon realized that few cities had the right climate or geography to host both events. So different cities were chosen for the Summer and Winter Games. This allowed cold-weather sports, such as skiing and ice-skating, to become Olympic events. The first Winter Olympics were attended by 294 athletes from 16 countries.

Coubertin died in May 1937. By then, the Olympics were a great success. It was obvious that they would be around for a long time.

Coubertin had been a rich man. But he had spent so much of his own money on the Olympics that he had none left when he died. Coubertin was buried in France. But his heart was cut out and buried beneath a memorial to him at Olympia.

Olympic Cities

1896 Athens, Greece
1900 Paris, France
1904 St. Louis, Missouri, U.S.A.
1908 London, England
1912 Stockholm, Sweden
1920 Antwerp, Belgium

In 1924, the Winter Games were added. Summer Games were held, or will be held, in the following cities.

1924 Paris, France
1928 Amsterdam, Netherlands
1932 Los Angeles, California, U.S.A.
1936 Berlin, Germany
1948 London, England
1952 Helsinki, Finland
1956 Melbourne, Australia
1960 Rome, Italy
1964 Tokyo, Japan
1968 Mexico City, Mexico
1972 Munich, Germany
1976 Montreal, Canada
1980 Moscow, Soviet Union
1984 Los Angeles, California, U.S.A.
1988 Seoul, South Korea
1992 Barcelona, Spain
1996 Atlanta, Georgia, U.S.A.
2000 Sydney, Australia
2004 Athens, Greece
2008 Beijing, China

Olympic Stadium, Montreal, Quebec, Canada

The Winter Games were held, or will be held, in the following cities.

1924 Chamonix, France
1928 St. Moritz, Switzerland
1932 Lake Placid, New York, U.S.A.
1936 Garmisch-Partenkirchen, Germany
1948 St. Moritz, Switzerland
1952 Oslo, Norway
1956 Cortina, Italy
1960 Squaw Valley, California, U.S.A.
1964 Innsbruck, Austria
1968 Grenoble, France
1972 Sapporo, Japan
1976 Innsbruck, Austria
1980 Lake Placid, New York, U.S.A.
1984 Sarajevo, Yugoslavia
1988 Calgary, Canada
1992 Albertville, France
1994 Lillehammer, Norway*
1998 Nagano, Japan
2002 Salt Lake City, Utah, U.S.A.
2006 Torino, Italy

Innsbruck, Austria

*In 1986, the IOC changed its rules to allow the Summer and Winter Games to be held in different years. The reason for this change was to allow television networks to sell more advertisements to be shown during the Olympic broadcasts. The 1994 Winter Games in Lillehammer were the first to follow this new schedule.

Olympic Traditions

The Olympic Rings: The rings symbolize excellence in sports around the world. They represent the five continents that participate in the Games (the Americas, Asia, Africa, Australia, and Europe). At least one of the five colors— blue, black, red, yellow, and green—is found in the flag of every nation in the world. 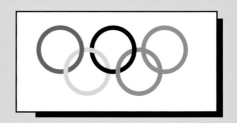 Coubertin thought of the idea for the Olympic rings after seeing a five-ring emblem on an altar in Delphi, Greece.

The Olympic Motto: The motto is *Citius*, *Altius*, *Fortius*. It is Latin for "Swifter, Higher, Stronger."

The Olympic Flame: The Olympic flame burns outside Olympia. About a year before the Olympics, a torch is lit from that flame. Then a series of relay runners carries the torch from Olympia to the Olympic host city. At the opening ceremonies, the torch is used to light an Olympic flame. It will burn throughout the Games. This tradition began in Germany before the 1936 Summer  Games. Until 1952, only the Summer Games had torch relays.

The Olympic Flag: The Olympic flag shows the five Olympic rings on a white background. The flag flies in the middle of the main stadium where the Games are held. At the end of the Olympics, the mayor of the host city passes the flag to the mayor of the city that will host the next Games. Baron de Coubertin designed the Olympic flag. The flag flew for the first time at the 1920 Olympics in Antwerp, Belgium.

The Parade of Athletes: During the opening ceremonies of every Olympics, the athletes march in by country. Greece is always the first country. Its position honors its status as the first host of the modern Olympics. The host nation enters last. All the other nations enter in alphabetical order in the language of the host country. During the closing ceremonies, the athletes march in as one group. This symbolizes the community of athletes rather than individual nations.

Mascots: The first unofficial Olympic **mascot** appeared at the 1968 Winter Games in Grenoble, France. Schuss was a cartoonlike character on skis. The first official mascot was Waldi, a dachshund who represented the 1972 Summer Games in Munich, Germany. Since 1972, almost every Olympics has had at least one mascot. Mascots are usually cartoon characters or animals connected to the host country. For example, Sam the Eagle was the mascot of the 1984 Summer Games in Los Angeles. The mascots at the 2000 Summer Games in Sydney, Australia, were an **echidna** named Millie, Ollie the kookaburra, and a platypus named Syd.

CHAPTER THREE

When the Olympics Come to Town

The Olympics have changed dramatically since the early days. Hosting the Olympics is a great honor. Cities all over the world work hard to win an Olympic bid. But being chosen to host the Olympics is only the beginning of a long, expensive, and complicated journey. How are cities chosen to host the Games? Why do they want to? And how do they prepare for the enormous event that the Olympics are today?

Olympic Committees at Work

The process of choosing an Olympic host city begins many years before the Games are held there. Each country has a national Olympic committee. These national committees receive bids from different cities that want to host the Olympics.

fun fact

The United States Olympics Committee, or USOC, received bids from eight different cities to host the 2012 Summer Games. These cities were Dallas, Houston, Tampa Bay, San Francisco, Los Angeles, New York City, Cincinnati, and Baltimore-Washington, D.C.

Inside the Olympic Stadium, Los Angeles, California, 1984

Each city's bid contains information on where events will be held. Some events are scheduled in places that already exist. These include stadiums, college pools and tracks, public beaches, and parks. Plans for building new facilities are also included.

The cities must also describe where the athletes will be housed during the Games. They must outline how athletes and spectators will travel to and from the events. Often, new bus routes, train lines, and roads must be built. Cities must also explain how athletes and spectators will be protected, both on and off the field.

Bids usually include a written description of the plans, as well as one or more videos. Members of the national committee visit each city, tour the area, and talk with the organizers about their plans.

Finally, the committee picks the city it thinks would make the best host. This city's bid is submitted to the IOC. The IOC then has many different world cities to consider.

The IOC Makes Its Choice

The IOC usually has about 10 cities from which to choose. Just as the individual countries' Olympic committees did, the IOC looks at each bid. It considers which city has the best athletic facilities, transportation, security, and housing plans. But the IOC must take many other factors into account.

The IOC tries to award Olympic bids to different parts of the world. It does not like to award the Olympics to the same continent more than once every few years.

Olympic cities are supposed to be chosen strictly on their ability to host the Games. However, other factors enter into the

Mitt Romney, Salt Lake City Olympic Organization Committee CEO, talks with the press, 2001

decision. One of the most important in recent years has been that of human rights.

In 1993, Beijing, China, was one of the choices to host the 2000 Summer Olympics. However, in 1989, the Chinese government had crushed a pro-democracy movement in Beijing's Tiananmen Square.

The IOC—and the rest of the world—was very concerned about human rights abuses in China. Because of this, China lost its chance to host the 2000 Olympics by two votes.

Beijing later won the 2008 Olympics. The Chinese government had made many promises to improve human rights and other conditions for its people.

After it reviews all the bids, the IOC narrows the choices. The committee now has three to five cities from which to choose. Members of the IOC visit each city several times. They go over the plans for the Olympics with city officials and local committee members.

The review process takes several years. Finally, the IOC meets to discuss and vote on the bids. This meeting takes place seven years before the actual Olympics. For example, the 2008 Olympics were awarded in 2001. The bids are awarded early enough to give the host city enough time to prepare. And preparing for the Olympics is a huge job!

Building an Olympic Dream

Once a city wins the chance to hold the Olympics, it still has a lot of work to do. When Barcelona won the 1992 Summer Olympics, it had to provide facilities for 257 events in 25 sports. It had to find housing for more than 10,000 athletes and judges. Also, 15,000 journalists and about 2 million spectators from around the world were expected!

When it won the 2008 Olympic bid, Beijing began China's greatest building project since the construction of the Great Wall. A new Olympic Park will be built just outside the city. It will contain sites for 15 different sports, including an 80,000-seat stadium. Beijing also plans to build an athletes' village in the Olympic Park. This village will house more than 17,000 athletes.

Construction of the stadium for the Olympic Games in Atlanta, Georgia

The Chinese government plans to spend billions of dollars to improve roads and public transportation. It also will spend $12 billion to clean Beijing's polluted air. In addition, the city will add about 45,000 hotel rooms to accommodate all the tourists who will come to the Games. Officials even plan to plant tens of thousands of trees to create an 1800-acre Olympic forest.

All this building requires a lot of money. Manchester, England, promised to build $84 million worth of new sports facilities when it bid on the 2000 Olympics. Manchester lost this bid to Sydney, Australia.

The 1976 Summer Games cost the city of Montreal almost $1.4 billion. Most of that bill was paid by taxpayers in Montreal and Quebec Province.

If hosting the Olympics costs so much, why do cities want to do it? Hosting the Olympics is a tremendous honor for a city. Athletes and spectators also spend millions of dollars when they visit the city during the Games. Atlanta estimates that hosting the 1996 Summer Games added $4.4 billion to the state's economy. It also gave Atlanta more than $500 million worth of new sports facilities.

Hosting the Olympics also means that billions of people around the world will see the city on television. This can lead to increased tourism in the future. Also, building new sports facilities and housing makes life better for city residents. It can also make unsafe or unhealthy places beautiful. For example, Sydney, Australia, converted a polluted landfill called Homebush Bay into sports facilities and an Olympic village for the athletes.

Beginning with the 1984 Summer Olympics in Los Angeles, businesses have been allowed to help pay expenses through advertising and sponsorship.

fun fact

Many of the people who work at the Olympics are volunteers. Barcelona used almost 10,000 volunteers during the 1992 Olympic Games. Sydney had 47,000 volunteers helping out during the 2000 Olympics. And Beijing plans to have 600,000 volunteers when it hosts the Summer Games in 2008!

Life in the Olympic Village

One of the most interesting places at the Olympics is the village where the athletes live. The first Olympic village was built for the 1932 Summer Games in Los Angeles, California. This village covered 250 acres and consisted of rows of two-room cottages. It had its own post office, hospital, police station, and firehouse. Only men lived in this Olympic village. Female athletes were housed in a Los Angeles hotel.

Athletes in today's Olympic villages usually live in **dormitories**. They eat their meals in a main dining hall. Exercise facilities, entertainment areas, and places where athletes can log on to the Internet are also available.

Montreal Olympic village dormitory

After the Games

What happens to the Olympic facilities after the Games are over? First, they are used for another major athletic event. About ten days after the Olympics end, the Paralympics are held on the same site.

The Paralympics are Olympic Games for disabled athletes. Like the Olympics, they are held every four years. Disabled athletes from around the world compete in events such as archery, basketball, wheelchair racing, cycling, weightlifting,

**11th Paralympics Summer Games
wheelchair race in Sydney, Australia**

soccer, swimming, skiing, ice-**sledge** hockey, ice-sledge racing, and more. The first Paralympics were held in 1960.

After the Paralympics, the facilities are used by the residents of the host city. For example, the Atlanta Braves baseball team now plays in part of Atlanta's Olympic Stadium. Housing for the athletes in Atlanta was turned into dormitories for students at Georgia Tech, a local college. Other cities have transformed their Olympic villages into low-cost housing.

CHAPTER FOUR

The Darker Side of the Olympics

The Olympic Games are supposed to be about athletic achievement. The focus of the Games is always on sports. But many Olympics have been marred by violence, political unrest, and tragedy. At times, wars have prevented the Olympics from being held at all.

Missing Games

Five Olympic Games have been canceled because of war. In 1916, the Games were scheduled to be held in Berlin, Germany. However, from 1914 to 1918, most of the world was fighting World War I.

Unlike the ancient Games, no truce was called to end the fighting during the Olympics. World War I made it impossible for Berlin to host the Games or for other countries to attend them. The Games were canceled. Berlin finally was chosen to host the Olympics in 1936.

World War II began in 1939 and lasted until 1945. Once again, fighting caused the cancellation of the Olympics. The 1940 Summer Games were scheduled for Tokyo, Japan. The Winter Games were to be held in Sapporo, Japan. The 1944 Summer Games were to be held in London, England. And the 1944 Winter Games were scheduled for Cortina, Italy.

After the war, all of these cities hosted the Games. London was the site of the first postwar Games in the summer of 1948. Cortina hosted the Winter Games in 1956. Tokyo held the 1964 Summer Games. And Sapporo hosted the 1972 Winter Games.

Boycotts

Other Olympics have been held as scheduled, but nations have boycotted the Games because of political concerns. Perhaps the most famous boycott occurred at the 1980 Summer Olympics in Moscow, the capital of the then Soviet Union.

fun fact

The losers of World War I (Germany, Austria, Bulgaria, Turkey, and Hungary) were not invited to attend the 1920 Olympics. Germany and Japan were not allowed at the London Games in 1948. They had lost World War II.

In December 1979, the Soviet Union invaded Afghanistan. To protest the war, U.S. President Jimmy Carter refused to allow U.S. athletes to attend the Games. More than 45 other countries, including Canada, Great Britain, and Australia, asked their athletes not to attend.

The 1980 Olympics went on as scheduled. However, in 1984, the Soviet Union and many other Communist countries boycotted the Summer Games in Los Angeles.

The 1980 boycott was not the first—or the last—in Olympic history. In 1956, Egypt, Iraq, the Netherlands, and Spain refused to send athletes to the Olympics as a protest against military actions taken by other nations who did attend the Games.

In 1976, thirty-two African nations asked the IOC to ban New Zealand from entering the Olympics. The African nations wanted New Zealand banned because its rugby team had toured South Africa. South Africa had been banned from Olympic competition because of their **segregated** system of laws called *apartheid*. The IOC refused to ban New Zealand because rugby was not an Olympic sport. Tanzania and other African nations, along with Guyana and Iraq, stayed home.

In 1988, the Summer Games were held in Seoul, South Korea. This angered North Korea, a longtime enemy of South Korea. North Korea boycotted the 1988 Games. So did Cuba, Ethiopia, and Nicaragua.

Boycotts win publicity for their supporters. But they are generally not successful. The Olympics are held anyway, whether all countries choose to come or not.

Boycotts also harm athletes. These competitors have spent years training for the Olympics. They are angry and hurt when their governments tell them they cannot participate. For these reasons, large-scale boycotts are probably a thing of the past.

fun fact

Russian officials were very upset during
the 2002 Winter Games in Salt Lake City,
Utah. They did not win many medals.
They were especially angered when the
Russian pairs figure skaters had to share
their gold medal with a Canadian couple
after a judging scandal. Russia threatened
to pull out of the closing ceremonies as a
protest. South Korea also threatened to
skip the closing ceremoines after their top
speed skater was disqualified from a race.
However, both countries did show up for
the closing ceremonies.

Russian gold medal figure skaters, 2002

The Hitler Games

In 1936, the Olympics were used by a government for political reasons. Five years earlier, the Summer Games had been awarded to Berlin, the capital of Germany. Adolf Hitler and the Nazi Party came to power in 1933.

Adolf Hitler

Hitler and the Nazis believed the white race was superior to all other races and **ethnic** groups. The Nazi government passed laws that **discriminated** against Jews; gypsies; and nonwhite, non-Christian groups. One Nazi Party newspaper went so far as to demand that the Berlin Olympic Games be open to whites only.

Many countries asked the IOC to move the Games to another city. The IOC refused. The Summer Games went on as scheduled in Berlin.

fun fact

Because of Germany's policies, a smaller effort was made by some countries to boycott the 1936 Winter Games in Garmisch-Partenkirchen, Germany.

Despite their **racist** views, Hitler and other Nazi Party members promised to welcome athletes of every race and ethnic group. They knew that if they didn't, the IOC might move the Games to another country.

Hitler turned the Olympics into a spectacular show. He wanted to impress the rest of the world with how beautiful and powerful Germany was. His goal was to show off the Nazi ideal of a "master race." However, Hitler's plans failed.

Even though German athletes won most of the medals at the Games, the most famous Olympian of the 1936 Games was an African American track-and-field star named Jesse Owens.

Owens was the first athlete to win four medals at one Olympics. He became a hero to most of the other athletes and the German people. Owens and the other nine African American members of the U.S. track-and-field team combined to win seven gold, three silver, and three bronze medals. Hitler's dream of white German athletes dominating the Olympics was destroyed.

Jesse Owens, the first athlete to win four medals at one Olympics

Political Protests

Sometimes it is the athletes themselves, not the governments, who want to make a political statement at the Olympics. That's what happened at the 1968 Summer Games in Mexico City. At that time, the United States was torn by racial turmoil. African Americans were struggling to win an equal place with whites in society.

Tommie Smith and John Carlos were two African American sprinters on the U.S. track team. Smith won a gold medal in the 200-meter race. Carlos won the bronze in the same event. The two men stood on the awards **podium**, listening to the American national anthem. Suddenly, they raised their black-gloved, clenched fists in a salute to "Black Power." Smith and Carlos were immediately stripped of their medals, thrown off the team, and sent home for their peaceful protest.

Black Power

Stokely Carmichael was a young black **activist** during the 1960s. He coined the phrase "Black Power." Many, including Dr. Martin Luther King Jr., felt Black Power was not the way to fight segregation. Black Power urged blacks to unite and end segregation by any means possible—even violence.

The Mexico City Olympics were also the scenes of riots against the Mexican government. Ten days before the Games began, government troops fired on a crowd of unarmed students. Hundreds were killed. Despite the violence, the Olympics went on as planned.

Changes at Barcelona

Most political events connected with the Olympics have caused anger or sorrow. But at the 1992 Summer Games in Barcelona, political changes led to many new Olympic competitors. Between 1989 and 1991, the Soviet Union and other Communist countries in Eastern Europe became democratic governments. This led the Soviet Union to break into 15 separate nations. Twelve of these nations, including Russia, competed as the "Unified Team." The other three countries—Estonia, Latvia, and Lithuania—competed as independent nations.

Athletes from all over the world cover the field during the opening cermonies at the Barcelona Games.

The Soviet Union was not the only country affected by the fall of Communism. Slovenia and Croatia competed as independent nations instead of with Yugoslavia. Athletes from Serbia, Montenegro, and Macedonia, which had also been part of Yugoslavia, competed as Independent Olympic Participants.

And for the first time since 1936, East and West Germany competed as one team instead of two. Germany became one nation again after the fall of the Berlin Wall in 1989.

The 1992 Games also saw the return of South Africa to Olympic competition. Since 1960, South Africa had not competed because of its system of apartheid. However, apartheid ended in 1990. So South Africa was welcomed back into the Olympic family.

fun fact

Because the Unified Team was not a separate country, it had no national anthem. Whenever an athlete from the Unified Team won the gold, a piece of classical music was played as the medal was awarded to the athlete.

Terrorist Tragedies

The most tragic and shocking event in Olympic history began on September 5, 1972. The Summer Games were being held in Munich, Germany. Early that morning, eight Palestinian terrorists broke into the Olympic village. They stormed into a dormitory housing athletes from Israel. An Israeli athlete and coach were killed. Nine members of the weightlifting and wrestling teams were taken **hostage**.

In exchange for the hostages' freedom, the terrorists demanded the release of 200 Palestinian prisoners held in Israeli jails. They also asked for a helicopter to fly them out of the country.

However, when the terrorists arrived at the airport, German troops opened fire. In the gun battle that followed, five terrorists, one policeman, and all nine athletes were killed.

The Olympics were suspended for one day. Some 84,000 people attended a memorial service in the Olympic stadium.

Many people thought the Games should have been canceled. But the IOC was determined not to allow the terrorists to gain attention by stopping the Olympics. The Israeli and German governments agreed. So the Games went on.

Terrorists struck again in Atlanta in 1996. Just after midnight on July 27, a bomb exploded in Centennial Olympic Park, a public area for sports fans from all over the world. The bomb was hidden in a knapsack. One women was killed, and hundreds more were injured. A foreign journalist died of a heart attack after rushing to the scene.

Shortly before the bomb exploded, security guard Richard Jewell spotted the suspicious-looking backpack. He quickly began moving people from the area.

At first, Jewell was hailed a hero. Not long afterward, he was accused of being the bomber. However, Jewell was later cleared of all charges.

The Olympic Park bomber still hasn't been found. Authorities believe the bombing was linked to two other bombings in Atlanta earlier in 1996.

The terrorist attacks of 1972 and 1996 have led to increased security at Olympic events. It is a solemn reminder that even in the world of sports, violence and politics are never far away.

CHAPTER FIVE

The Shadow of Drugs

The Olympics are supposed to show athletes at their strongest, fastest, and fittest. Achieving a place on the Olympic team is the high point of many athletes' lives and careers. These athletes know that if they win a medal, they will go into the record books and become famous. For this reason, many athletes take drugs in order to perform better.

Some drugs are injected into the athlete's bloodstream. Others are taken in pill form. Some are even produced naturally by the body. Others are created from chemicals in a laboratory. But no matter how they are taken or where they come from, using any kind of performance-enhancing drug is strictly against Olympic rules.

In the early days of the Olympics, drugs were not a big problem. However, by the middle of the 20th century, it was no secret that some athletes were improving their performances by **artificial** means. In many cases, athletes were told to take drugs by their coaches, trainers, and doctors.

Many athletes even took drugs because their governments told them to! This was especially true in Communist countries.

There, the athletic programs were controlled and paid for by the government.

In 1968, Olympic athletes began taking drug tests. Today, any athlete who wins a medal or sets a record has to provide a urine sample. Other athletes are chosen **at random** to take drug tests. These samples are **analyzed** for substances that have been banned by the IOC. Athletes are also tested several weeks before the Olympics.

Between 1968 and 1988, forty-three Olympic athletes were disqualified because of failed drug tests. However, testing did little to stop athletes from using drugs.

Instead, some competitors switched to drugs that would not show up on the tests. Other athletes stopped taking drugs a few weeks before the Olympics. Traces of the drugs could not be found in the body after several weeks.

During the 1960s and 1970s, many Western athletes wondered about competitors from Communist countries, such as East Germany. Many East German female swimmers had powerful muscles and broad shoulders. They almost looked like men instead of women! Many people accused these athletes of taking **steroids** to change their bodies and improve their performances.

The East German team and government strongly denied these charges. Meanwhile, it was hard for athletes from other countries to compete against these "super athletes." The East German team won 411 medals between 1968 and 1988.

After the fall of Communism in the early 1990s, former members of East Germany's athletic program finally admitted the truth. East German athletes *had* taken steroids and other performance-enhancing drugs. Athletes from other Communist countries also revealed that they had taken drugs before the Games.

Communist athletes weren't the only ones

who used drugs to improve their performances. One of the biggest scandals in Olympic history occurred during the 1988 Summer Games in Seoul, Korea. During those games, Canadian star athlete Ben Johnson set a record when he won a gold medal in the 100-meter dash.

A few hours later, Johnson failed a drug test. His gold medal was taken away and given to the silver medalist, Carl Lewis from the United States.

Ben Johnson

Johnson was also banned from competition for several years.

Later, Johnson admitted he had used steroids and growth hormones for most of his career. He begged other athletes not to cheat the way he had.

Drugs continued to be a problem in the 1990s and beyond. Before and during the 2000 Summer Games, many athletes were disqualified for drug use. These athletes included the entire Bulgarian weightlifting team, a teenage Romanian gymnast, 40 Chinese athletes from various sports, and American shot-putter C. J. Hunter.

Blood Doping

Taking drugs isn't the only way athletes cheat. Some athletes have some of their blood removed a few weeks before a competition. Oxygen is pumped into the blood. Then the blood is injected back into the athlete's body. Because the blood has extra oxygen, the athlete has more **endurance** and can perform better. Even though blood doping doesn't use any banned drugs, it is still illegal in Olympic competition.

Using performance-enhancing drugs is harmful in many ways. Taking any kind of illegal drug can hurt the body. Even if a drug makes a person stronger or faster, it can later lead to serious health problems. For example, using steroids can cause serious damage to a person's heart and liver.

Taking drugs also harms other athletes because it's a form of cheating. Athletes who use drugs have an unfair advantage over their competitors.

Drugs have other harmful effects. Today, many people suspect an athlete has taken drugs any time he or she achieves a new record. The athlete might be completely innocent, yet his or her reputation is damaged. For example, many rumors were passed around that Florence Griffith Joyner used drugs to achieve her incredible records on the track. However, Griffith Joyner passed every drug test and always insisted she had never taken drugs.

Will there ever be athletic competitions without drugs? Probably not. The desire to win is just too strong to prevent some athletes from cheating to achieve their goals.

CHAPTER SIX

The Future of the Olympics

Over the past few years, the Olympics have faced a great deal of questions. Many aspects of the Games still have problems.

Amateur or Professional?

From the beginning, the modern Olympics were for amateur athletes. Baron Pierre de Coubertin felt that athletes should compete because they loved a sport, not because they were paid. Throughout Olympic history, professional athletes have been strictly forbidden to take part. However, the meaning of the word *amateur* has changed over the years.

During the 1920s, some U.S. athletes were accused of not being amateurs because they accepted **scholarships**. During the 1930s, physical education teachers could not take part because they were paid for athletic activities. In the eyes of the IOC, this made them professionals.

Jim Thorpe and the Lost Medals

In 1912, twenty-four-year-old U.S. track-and-field star Jim Thorpe won two gold medals at the Stockholm Olympics. King Gustav V of Sweden called him "the greatest athlete in the world." It was one of the proudest moments in Thorpe's life.

But less than a year later, Thorpe's glory changed to shame. A reporter discovered that many years earlier, Thorpe had been paid $25 a week to play minor-league baseball. Under the rules of the day, that meant Thorpe was a professional athlete.

Despite protests from Thorpe and the American people, his medals were taken away. His name was also removed from the Olympic record books.

In 1943, Thorpe's supporters began a campaign to win back his medals. The campaign continued even after Thorpe died in 1953.

Finally in 1982, the IOC named Thorpe an Olympic athlete once again. Thorpe's name was put back in the record books, and his gold medals were returned to his family.

When Communist countries entered the Olympics, the difference between amateurs and professionals became even more unclear. Communist governments supported their athletes while they trained. This meant that Communist countries could create very strong teams. Meanwhile, athletes from the United States, Canada, and other democratic countries often struggled to train for their sports while working to support themselves and their families.

Corporate **sponsorship** also created questions about what defined a professional athlete. Was an athlete a professional if he or she received clothing or equipment from a sponsor? Some people thought that receiving free items was a form of payment. Others said only athletes who were paid to compete could be called professional.

Other athletes received thousands of dollars to appear at events or give speeches. These athletes weren't being paid for playing a sport. But they were receiving money because of their athletic abilities. Did that make them professionals?

Finally in 1981, the IOC changed its rules about who could compete. Now it would be up to the governing body of each individual sport to decide if professional athletes could participate.

This change led to a variety of standards. Some sports allowed athletes to place money in **trust funds**. They could use the funds to support themselves and still be considered amateurs. The International Tennis Federation said that any teenage players would be considered amateurs, no matter how much money they earned.

Other sports allowed professionals to join Olympic teams. In 1992, professional players from the National Basketball Association were allowed to play on the U.S. Olympic team. The U.S. team overwhelmed all the other competitors. The team became known as the Dream Team. In 1998, professionals from the National Hockey League played on teams from the United States, Canada, Russia, the Czech Republic, Sweden, and Finland.

Opinions differ about whether professional athletes should be allowed to compete in the Olympics. Some feel that using professional athletes allows countries to create the strongest teams they can. Others say that **showcasing** superstar athletes makes the Olympics even more popular. However, opponents say that using professionals makes it harder for young amateurs to take part in the Olympics.

Commercialism

The Olympics have also been accused of becoming too commercial. The 1984 Summer Games in Los Angeles were the first to use money from private companies to pay for the Games. Companies, such as McDonald's and Kodak, paid millions of dollars or donated products and services to be an "official sponsor" of the Games. McDonald's was even allowed to run a promotion in which free food was given away every time a U.S. athlete won a medal. Because of corporate sponsorship, the 1984 Olympics made a profit of more than $200 million.

The 1996 Olympics in Atlanta were even more commercial. Companies paid up to $40 million to be an Olympic sponsor. Some of these sponsorships seemed to have little to do with the Games. For example, it's hard to understand why the Olympics need an "official game show."

Many people criticize commercial sponsorship because it takes away from the athletic events. It turns the Olympics into just another advertising campaign.

However, private sponsorship helps host cities pay the huge expenses of holding the Olympics. It helps build better facilities for athletes and spectators. As the cost to host the Games increases, it seems likely that corporate sponsorship and other commercial enterprises will continue to be part of the Olympic experience.

Scandal at the IOC

The International Olympic Committee faced one of its toughest challenges in 1999. That year, it was revealed that members of the IOC had been bribed to award the 2002 Winter Olympics to Salt Lake City, Utah.

Between 1992 and 1998, the Salt Lake City Olympic Committee awarded thousands of dollars in scholarships to children of IOC members. A Utah health-care organization donated $28,000 in services, including cosmetic surgery, to IOC members. Other expensive gifts also came to light.

News about Salt Lake City's bribes prompted similar stories from other cities. One newspaper reported that the committee running Anchorage, Alaska's bid for the Games had been asked for $30,000 for IOC members in 1992 and 1994. The Anchorage committee refused—and did not win the right to host the Games.

Another news story claimed that Switzerland was considering giving a $1.5 million tax break to the IOC at the same time one of its cities was bidding on the 2006 Winter Games. These Games were eventually awarded to Torino, Italy.

In response to the bribery scandal, the IOC began an investigation of its practices. Stricter rules and policy changes followed the investigation. Several IOC members were forced to return gifts and repay money they had received.

The Lure of the Olympics

The Olympics have faced many problems. But they are still the most popular sports competition in the world and a truly global event.

Taking part in the Olympics—and even winning a medal or two—is a supreme honor. The Olympics let an athlete show the world that he or she is one of the best.

The Olympics can also be financially successful for athletes. Even if the athlete never has a professional career, a medal winner can make millions of dollars through product **endorsements** and personal appearances.

Nations also take pride in their Olympic athletes and their achievements. Lists of medal winners are printed in newspapers and announced on radio and television. Winners are given a hero's welcome when they return home. And, as we have seen, countries spend a tremendous amount of money, time, and effort just for the honor of having one of their cities host the Games.

Finally, and perhaps most importantly, the Olympics promote an ideal of sportsmanship and honor that still appeals to people around the world. The Games bring millions of people from different cultures together for a celebration of human effort and glory. Most of the athletes who compete in the Olympics know that they will never win a medal. These athletes compete for the glory of the sport. They compete to bring honor to themselves and their countries. In spite of scandals and controversies, it seems clear that the Olympics will continue to inspire and amaze for years to come.

Closing ceremonies, Sydney, Australia

Glossary

activist person who strongly supports or opposes an issue

amateur being involved in an activity or sport as a pastime, not as an occupation

analyze to study

archaeologist scientist who studies the past

arena enclosed area used for public entertainment

artificial produced by humans, not nature

at random chosen without definite aim, direction, rule, or pattern

boycott act of refusing to have dealings with another person or organization in order to show disapproval of certain conditions

bribe money or a gift given or promised that influences the judgment or conduct of a person

city-state self-governing state consisting of a city and surrounding territory

Communist one who believes in a government that owns all business and industry

decathlon athletic contest consisting of ten track-and-field events

defect to leave one country for another because of political reasons

discus disk that is hurled for distance in track-and-field events

discriminate to treat someone differently because he or she belongs to a minority group

disqualify to prevent someone from taking part in an activity, usually because he or she broke a rule

dormitory residence hall providing rooms for individuals or groups, usually without individual baths

dumbbell short bar with weights at each end

echidna type of spiny anteater found in Australia

endorsement act of publicly supporting the use of a product

endurance ability to withstand stressful effort or activity

equestrian having to do with horseback riding

ethnic relating to large groups of people classed according to common racial, national, tribal, religious, or cultural origins

excavate to dig up

herald official of a tournament who makes the announcements

hostage person taken by force to secure the taker's demands

javelin slender spear that is thrown in track-and-field events

marathon long-distance race of 26 miles and 385 yards

mascot person, animal, or object adopted by a group as a symbol, usually to bring the group good luck

peddler one who offers merchandise for sale on the street

pentathlon athletic contest consisting of five track-and-field events

podium structure on which athletes stand to receive their medals

professional being engaged in an activity for pay

quarantine relating to the act of keeping an animal or person away from others to stop the spread of disease

racist having the belief that one race is better than all other races

remedy medicine or cure

revive to bring back

scholarship award that pays for higher education

segregate to separate by class, race, religion, or sex

showcasing showing off

sledge strong, heavy sled

sponsorship payment that allows for the completion of a project

steroid drug that builds strength and muscle mass

strychnine bitter poison from the nightshade plant

terrorist relating to the use of violence to force a desired action

trust fund money set aside for a person to use for a specific purpose

Index